AFRICAN-AMERICAN MUSICIANS

CLAUDETTE HEGEL

TITLES IN THIS SERIES

AFRICAN-AMERICAN MUSICIANS

CLAUDETTE HEGEL

MASON CREST
PHILADELPHIA

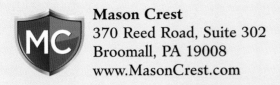

Mason Crest
370 Reed Road, Suite 302
Broomall, PA 19008
www.MasonCrest.com

Printed and bound in the United States of America.

CPSIA Compliance Information: Batch #MBC2012-4. For further information, contact Mason Crest at 1-866-MCP-Book.

First printing
1 3 5 7 9 8 6 4 2

Library of Congress Cataloging-in-Publication Data

Hegel, Claudette.
African-American musicians / by Claudette Hegel.
    p. cm. — (Major black contributions from emancipation to civil rights)
Includes bibliographical references and index.
ISBN 978-1-4222-2374-1 (hc)
ISBN 978-1-4222-2387-1 (pb)
1. African Americans—Music—History and criticism—Juvenile literature.
2. Popular music—United States—History and criticism—Juvenile literature.
3. African American musicians—Juvenile literature. I. Title.
ML3479.H44 2012
780.89'96073—dc23
                                    2011051949

Publisher's note: All quotations in this book are taken from original sources, and contain the spelling and grammatical inconsistencies of the original texts.

Picture credits: Library of Congress: 3, 8, 12, 13, 14, 16, 17, 18, 20, 21, 23, 25, 28, 29, 30, 31, 32, 37, 42; courtesy Motown Records: 45 (top); PR Newswire: 53; Arvzdix / Shutterstock.com: 54; Carl Bjorklund / Shutterstock.com: 57; S. Bukley / Shutterstock.com: 55; Carroteater / Shutterstock.com: 46; Helga Esteb / Shutterstock.com: 50; Featureflash / Shutterstock.com: 34, 45 (four lower images), 51; Mimmo Ferraro / Shutterstock.com: 40; Adam J. Sablich / Shutterstock.com: 7, 48; TDC Photography / Shutterstock.com: 36; U.S. Department of Defense: 43, 47.

TABLE OF CONTENTS

INTRODUCTION

Dr. Marc Lamont Hill

I t is impossible to tell the story of America without telling the story of Black Americans. From the struggle to end slavery, all the way to the election of the first Black president, the Black experience has been a window into America's own movement toward becoming a "more perfect union." Through the tragedies and triumphs of Blacks in America, we gain a more full understanding of our collective history and a richer appreciation of our collective journey. This book series, MAJOR BLACK CONTRIBUTIONS FROM EMANCIPATION TO CIVIL RIGHTS, spotlights that journey by showing the many ways that Black Americans have been a central part of our nation's development.

In this series, we are reminded that Blacks were not merely objects of history, swept up in the winds of social and political inevitability. Rather, since the end of legal slavery, Black men and women have actively fought for their own rights and freedoms. It is through their courageous efforts (along with the efforts of allies of all races) that Blacks are able to enjoy ever increasing levels of inclusion in American democracy. Through this series, we learn the names and stories of some of the most important contributors to our democracy.

But this series goes far beyond the story of slavery to freedom. The books in this series also demonstrate the various contributions of Black Americans to the nation's social, cultural, technological, and intellectual growth. While these books provide new and deeper insights into the lives and stories of familiar figures like Martin Luther King, Michael Jordan, and Oprah Winfrey, they also introduce readers to the contributions of countless heroes who have often been pushed to the margins of history. In reading this series, we are able to see that Blacks have been key contributors across every field of human endeavor.

Although this is a series about Black Americans, it is important and necessary reading for everyone. While readers of color will find enormous purpose and pride in uncovering the history of their ancestors, these books should also create similar sentiments among readers of all races and ethnicities. By understanding the rich and deep history of Blacks, a group often ignored or marginalized in history, we are reminded that everyone has a story. Everyone has a contribution. Everyone matters.

The insights of these books are necessary for creating deeper, richer, and more inclusive classrooms. More importantly, they remind us of the power and possibility of individuals of all races, places, and traditions. Such insights not only allow us to understand the past, but to create a more beautiful future.

A modest African-American church stands in the middle of a South Carolina cornfield, 1930s. In the southern states before the Civil War, black slaves who had been converted to Christianity developed a new way to worship through religious songs known as "spirituals." This uniquely African-American form of music would have a great influence on subsequent genres of American music.

1

WELLSPRINGS

Music has always been an important part of people's lives. It provides a powerful way to express our feelings. It helps us mark special occasions, whether they are happy (such as a wedding) or sad (such as a funeral).

Of course, music isn't just for special occasions. It is also a big part of everyday life. It entertains. It can inspire us as we work or exercise. It can be an enjoyable background as we relax by ourselves or hang out with friends.

AFRICAN AMERICANS AND AMERICAN MUSIC

American music has been shaped by many influences. That's hardly surprising. The country was settled by waves of immigrants from around the world. These immigrants brought with them the culture of their old lands, including distinct musical traditions. In America, the various traditions met and blended. Over time, new forms of musical expression emerged.

African Americans played a vital role in this process. Popular musical genres (types) such as jazz, blues, rock 'n' roll, and hip-hop were pioneered by African-American musicians. These genres tapped elements of the rich musical traditions of Africa. And they grew—at least in part—out of the unique experience of blacks in America.

Unlike other groups of immigrants, blacks didn't come to America willingly. Between the early 1600s and the early 1800s, an estimated 2 million black Africans were brought to American shores as slaves. Emancipation—the freeing of the slaves—occurred as a result of the Civil War. But emancipation didn't mean equality for African Americans. The Civil War ended in 1865. Yet for another hundred years, laws and unwritten social rules, especially in the South, kept black people from participating fully in American society.

Discrimination may have been worst in the South, but racism existed throughout the country. Many whites assumed that blacks didn't have much to offer the wider American culture. Yet white audiences would come to embrace music to which African Americans had contributed heavily. Sometimes this mainstream acceptance occurred only after white performers had adopted musical styles first introduced by African Americans.

AFRICAN-AMERICAN MUSIC DURING SLAVERY

The Africans who crossed the Atlantic Ocean chained together in the holds of slave ships came from different parts of Africa. They belonged to different tribes. They spoke a variety of languages. Their cultures, including their music, were diverse.

The conditions of slavery largely erased these cultural differences, however. A blended African-American culture evolved in colonial North America and, after the Revolutionary War, the United States.

African-American music included key features of African musical traditions. One was the repetition of short phrases throughout a song. Another was call-and-response. In this musical form, a leader would sing, chant, or play a phrase, and a group would respond with a different phrase. Still another feature was the use of complex, often layered rhythms. In Africa,

drums produced these rhythms. But most slaveholders in the United States forbade their slaves to play drums, fearing that drumbeats could serve as a signal for a slave uprising. So instead of drums, slaves produced percussive sounds by tapping on whatever objects were available, including their own bodies. These and other musical features that slaves adopted from African music would later greatly influence the development of American popular music.

There were several types of early African-American songs. Slaves sang "work songs" or "field hollers" while toiling in the fields. Many of these songs had a call-and-response format. The rhythm helped slaves work together.

African-American Music Appreciation Month

President Barack Obama declared June 2010 African-American Music Appreciation Month. "Music can tell a story, assuage our sorrows, provide blessing and redemption, and express a soul's sublime and powerful beauty," the president said.

It inspires us daily, giving voice to the human spirit. For many, including the African-American community, music unites individuals through a shared heritage. During African-American Music Appreciation Month, we celebrate the extraordinary legacy of African-American singers, composers, and musicians, as well as their indelible contributions to our Nation and our world.

Throughout our history, African-American music has conveyed the hopes and hardships of a people who have struggled, persevered, and overcome. Through centuries of injustice, music comforted slaves, fueled a cultural renaissance, and sustained a movement for equality.

Slaves plant sweet potatoes on a South Carolina plantation, circa 1862. "Work songs" helped relieve the boredom of tedious farm jobs, and also provided a rhythm that helped the slaves do their work more efficiently.

During times when slaves were not working, music remained an important part of their lives. Like other people, they gathered together and made music for entertainment. Fiddles and banjos (which were homemade and may have been inspired by a traditional West African instrument) were often used for accompaniment. Folktales served as frequent subjects of songs.

But perhaps the most significant inspiration for early African-American songs was Christianity. The 1700s saw a revival of Christian religious belief among whites in North America. This movement was known as the Great Awakening. White preachers worked to win converts, including free and enslaved African Americans. Many slaves found great comfort in the Christian message. It said that all people were equal before God. It promised salvation. Bible stories such as the Jewish people's deliverance from slavery in Egypt had special significance.

As they adopted Christianity, African-American slaves wrote their own religious songs, called spirituals. These songs were highly expressive. Many referred to Bible stories that promised freedom and a better future.

Spirituals often had double meanings. Songs about the "Promised Land" didn't always mean Heaven. The singer might also mean the North, where blacks were allowed to live as free men and women. References to salvation could be about escaping from the plantation and reaching the safety of a northern city like Philadelphia or Boston, or even Canada. A lyric about "striking down the Pharaoh" could refer to a cruel plantation owner or overseer. Some music historians even believe the lyrics of spirituals carried hidden messages about secret meetings or directions for escape attempts.

The tunes and lyrics of spirituals changed often to meet the needs of the slaves who sang them. Spirituals weren't written down until after the Civil War. In 1867, William Allen, Lucy McKim Garrison, and Charles Ware collected lyrics and tunes for more than 100 spirituals and work songs. They published them in a book called *Slave Songs of the United States*. This was the first published collection of African-American music.

R. Nathaniel Dett (1882–1943) was a famous composer of the early 20th century. His arrangements of black folk songs and spirituals were very popular and are still played today.

THE FISK JUBILEE SINGERS

In the years after the Civil War, new schools were created to educate freed slaves and other young African Americans. One of these schools was Fisk University in Nashville, Tennessee. It opened in 1866. Five years later, however, Fisk was in deep financial trouble. The school barely had enough money to continue operating. To raise money, the school's music director created a nine-member choir. Beginning in October 1871, the group spent 18 months touring the United States. Revenue from performances helped keep the school operating.

The performances were held in northern states, like Ohio, Pennsylvania, New York, and Massachusetts. Many white people went to the concerts. The Fisk Jubilee Singers performed patriotic songs and ballads. But their program also included spirituals. For most audience members, this was the first time they had ever heard African-American music.

The Fisk Jubilee Singers were very popular. In 1872, President Ulysses S. Grant invited the group to sing at the White House. The singers later toured Europe, even giving a concert for England's Queen Victoria.

The Fisk University Singers' concerts raised more than $150,000. Some of the money was used to build Fisk University's first permanent building.

Members of the Fisk Jubilee Singers group pose in this photo taken in the 1870s.

That building, called Jubilee Hall, is still being used today.

The Fisk Jubilee Singers showed African Americans and their music in a positive light. The minstrel shows of the time did not.

MINSTREL SHOWS

Minstrel shows began in the 1830s. They proved very popular with white audiences. White actors would darken their skin with makeup called blackface. They would sing, dance, do skits, and tell jokes—all while portraying African-American characters. These characters represented ugly stereotypes of black people. For example, one popular minstrel character was Jim Crow. He was a happy and lazy slave. Another popular character was Zip Coon, a free black. He dressed in fine clothes and believed he was smart, but he always said stupid things. The minstrel shows made fun of African Americans as foolish, lazy, superstitious, or untrustworthy. Unfortunately, many white people who saw minstrel shows believed these racist stereotypes.

Minstrel shows continued after the Civil War. During this time, African-American performers began joining minstrel troupes. Minstrelsy was still highly popular, and black entertainers had few other opportunities to make a living. So they too donned blackface and acted out the old racist stereotypes that white audiences had come to expect.

Still, minstrel shows offered talented African-American performers a chance to show their skills. One such performer was songwriter James A. Bland (1854–1911). He was born to a family of free blacks in New York and was singing in minstrel shows by the time he was 14. After graduating from Howard College, an all-black school in Washington, D.C., he continued performing. Bland wrote more than 700 songs. One of them, "Oh, Dem Golden Slippers," is still played in parades. Another song, "Carry Me Back to Old Virginny," was Virginia's official state song from 1940 to 1997. Bland, who was sometimes called the "world's greatest minstrel man," is a member of the Songwriters Hall of Fame.

The popularity of blackface minstrel shows declined in the 1870s and 1880s. But these shows continued into the 20th century.

The cover for sheet music to three of James A. Bland's songs, published in 1879. Bland's portrait appears in the lower circle on the sheet music.

RAGTIME

During the 1870s and 1880s, many concert bands were formed in the United States. These bands featured brass horns, as well as drums and cymbals. Concert bands played the different types of music that were popular at the time: marches, waltzes, hymns, patriotic songs such as "America the Beautiful," and sentimental ballads like "Molly Malone." Blacks as well as whites formed concert bands and performed locally.

By the mid-1890s, some black musicians were combining the rhythms of marches with traditional African-American music to create something new. The new music had a "ragged" sound, with a fast and happy beat. It became known as ragtime. Ragtime music was usually written for piano, but brass bands began to perform the new music as well. African-American composers like Scott Joplin and James Scott became famous for their ragtime compositions.

Joplin (ca. 1867–1917) was called "the King of Ragtime" for his many hit songs. When he performed at the Chicago World's Fair in 1893, he helped introduce ragtime to a national audience. The music soon became very popular. In 1899, Joplin published the song "Maple Leaf Rag." It became the first sheet music to sell a million copies. Some of his other well-known songs include "The Entertainer" (1902) and "The Pineapple Rag" (1903). Joplin's success made it easier for later African-American composers and musicians to reach audiences of all races.

Scott Joplin

Joplin inspired James Scott (1885–1938). Scott was a teenager working in a Missouri music store when his first song was published in 1903. Three years later, he moved to St. Louis, where he met Joplin. The famous composer introduced him to his sheet music publisher, John Stark. Scott's first ragtime song published by Stark, "Frog Legs Rag" (1906), was a big hit. Scott wrote many other great ragtime songs that were published by Stark over the next 16 years.

The popularity of ragtime music declined in the early 20th century. However, ragtime helped inspire two later forms of African-American music that would become very popular during the 20th century: blues and jazz.

This sheet music cover to a Scott Joplin ragtime song published in 1899 includes an African-American caricature of the type that was common in minstrel shows of the 19th century.

Statue of William Christopher "W. C." Handy in his hometown of Florence, Alabama. The influential songwriter and composer is known as the "Father of the Blues."

2

SINGING THE BLUES

By the late 19th century, some African-American musicians—especially in the South—were mixing elements of work songs and spirituals to create a new sound. As this music evolved, it took several distinctive characteristics. It had a strong rhythm. It usually had a 12-bar structure. It employed flat notes at specific intervals of a musical scale. Frequently, the lyrics were arranged into three-line stanzas, with the second line repeating the first. And the lyrics often expressed pain, sadness, and suffering. The music was called the blues.

THE BEGINNING OF THE BLUES

In 1903, an African-American musician and bandleader named W. C. Handy (1873–1958) fell asleep while waiting for a train in Tutwiler, Mississippi. The sound of a man singing and playing a guitar woke him. Handy later said it was "the weirdest music I had ever heard."

Handy, a native of Alabama, was already interested in the African-American folk music of Mississippi. He found that he couldn't get the unusual sound out of his mind. Over the next few years, he worked on songs that employed not just the brass instruments used by his band, but also guitars, banjos, fiddles, and pianos.

In 1909, Handy and his band moved to Memphis, Tennessee. That year,

W. C. Handy

a local politician named E. H. Crump hired Handy to write a song for his campaign. After the song helped Crump win election as mayor, Handy changed the words and renamed it "Memphis Blues." The song was published as sheet music in 1912. Its success introduced blues music to a wider audience.

Handy wrote many other great blues songs, such as "St. Louis Blues" (1914) and "Beale Street Blues" (1916). He proved to be a smart businessman as well as a great composer and bandleader. Handy joined an African-American entrepreneur named Harry Pace to form a music publishing company. He was then able to make more money from the songs he wrote and performed. Today, W. C. Handy is known as "the Father of the Blues."

BLUES MUSIC BREAKS OUT

Other African-American musicians made a living by performing blues music. In 1920, a singer named Mamie Smith (1883–1946) made a record that included a song called "Crazy Blues." This was the first recording of a blues song. Smith's record was a big hit, selling more than a million copies. Record companies saw a new way to make money. They rushed to record other African-American blues singers.

Between 1923 and 1928, singer Gertrude "Ma" Rainey (1886–1939) recorded more than 100 blues songs. She was a performer who had been touring the country for many years on the vaudeville circuit. Vaudeville shows included a hodgepodge of entertainment acts, including music, dance, comedy, magic, and trained animals. The success of Rainey's blues records enabled her to retire from vaudeville. She managed two

— Did You Know? —

Before W. C. Handy, early blues artists rarely put their songs down on paper. Instead, they passed the songs on to others by playing them during their travels.

Bessie Smith was the most popular blues singer of the 1920s. Her distinctive vocal style had a major influence on many later singers, including Billie Holiday, Mahalia Jackson, and Aretha Franklin.

theaters in Georgia that she had bought with her earnings.

One of Ma Rainey's former dancers, Bessie Smith (1894–1937), was even more successful as a blues singer. During the 1920s, Smith recorded more than 160 songs for Columbia Records. She was often joined by some of the best African-American musicians of the time. These included trumpeter Louis Armstrong, piano player James P. Johnson, and trombonist Charlie Green. Smith was nicknamed "Empress of the Blues." She was the highest-paid African-American entertainer of the 1920s.

Lemon Jefferson (1893–1929) was another well-known blues singer. He was born blind but learned how to play the guitar when he was a teenager. In 1926, Blind Lemon Jefferson became the first bluesman to record a solo album at a major studio, Paramount Records. The studio made him change his song lyrics a little so they would appeal to a white audience. Blind Lemon's style of music became known as the Texas blues. During his career he sometimes worked with other famous blues performers from Texas such as Huddie "Lead Belly" Ledbetter (1888–1949) and Aaron "T-Bone" Walker (1910–1975).

Singer and guitar player Robert Johnson (1911–1938) was a master of the Delta blues style that arose is northwest Mississippi. Johnson traveled through the small towns of Mississippi, playing on street corners for tips. He recorded only about a dozen songs between 1936 and 1938, when he

— Did You Know? —

Many bluesmen of the South were too poor to buy instruments. Instead, they used objects such as washboards and jugs as instruments. The music they played was called "skiffle."

died suddenly at the age of 27. But his music had great influence on many blues performers, as well as later rock artists. British bands such as Led Zeppelin and the Rolling Stones recorded versions of his songs. Eric Clapton, widely recognized as one of the greatest guitarists in the history of rock music, once said that Johnson's music is "the finest music I have ever heard. I have always trusted its purity, and I always will." Clapton recorded two albums of Johnson's music.

BOOGIE-WOOGIE AND BARRELHOUSE MUSIC

Between 1910 and 1930, about 2 million African Americans moved from the South to cities in the North, Midwest, and West in what became known as the Great Migration. They wanted to escape racism and find good jobs.

The Great Migration helped bring the music of southern blacks to other parts of the country. In the process, the music evolved. For example, blues musicians in cities usually played faster and louder than musicians in rural areas. They had to do so if people were to hear their music above the noise in crowded nightclubs.

In the South, meanwhile, African Americans weren't allowed to go to the same clubs and saloons that whites frequented. Jim Crow laws, as they were called, required racial segregation in public places. Even in other parts of the country, black people were often not welcome in nightclubs with white patrons. To listen to music, dance, and drink, blacks had to go to clubs that catered to African Americans. In the South especially, this often meant a "barrelhouse"—which was sometimes nothing more than a shack or tent where alcohol was served. Barrelhouses usually couldn't afford to hire more than one musician. So piano players in these clubs

Huddie "Lead Belly" Ledbetter (1888–1949) mixed gospel, blues, folk, and country music into its own sound, country blues. He served several stints in prison, one of them in Louisiana starting in 1930. Lead Belly got out in 1934 after friends sent a record to Louisiana's governor. On one side was a petition for his release. On the other side was Lead Belly performing his classic song "Goodnight Irene." He is pictured here with his wife, Martha, in 1935.

learned to play in a vigorous style that sounded like many instruments at once. The pianos were often out of tune. Some people said the music sounded like a runaway train.

The name for this new style of music would come from a song by piano player Clarence "Pinetop" Smith. In 1928, Smith recorded "Pinetop's Boogie-Woogie." Boogie-woogie music was very popular in the 1930s and 1940s. In the 1950s, it would contribute to other musical forms, such as rockabilly and rock 'n' roll.

GOSPEL MUSIC

The word *gospel* means "good news." Christians use this word to refer to books about the life of Jesus. The Christian faith was an important part of African-American life. Gospel music, which had lyrics about spiritual matters, began during the 1870s in churches and especially at camp meetings. These were religious gatherings held outdoors in rural areas. Like the earlier spirituals, many songs at camp meetings included repeated phrases. These made it easier for people to learn the songs quickly.

Some Types of Blues Music

Music experts distinguish many categories of blues music. Some of the most popular forms include the following:

- **Delta blues** is typically performed by a single guitarist, rather than by a group. Blind Lemon Jefferson and Robert Johnson were known for this style. Often, the guitarist will create the distinctive sound of Delta blues by sliding a bottleneck or other object up and down the strings.

- **Memphis blues** is performed by small "jug bands," sometimes playing homemade instruments. The music is upbeat and good for dancing. W. C. Handy helped make the Memphis blues sound popular.

- **Classic blues** has a smooth sound. Bessie Smith, Ma Rainey, and Mamie Smith sang classic blues.

- **Texas blues** features more guitar solos than other types of blues. T-Bone Walker and Johnny Copeland are two famous performers of Texas blues.

- **Chicago blues** mixes jazz and gospel sounds with electric guitars and amplified harmonicas, drums, and horns. Muddy Waters, B. B. King, and Howlin' Wolf (Chester Arthur Burnett) are notable examples of Chicago bluesmen.

- **Vaudeville blues**, or jazz blues, is often played by a small jazz combo. Billie Holiday, Louis Armstrong, and Ella Fitzgerald all performed in this style.

- **British blues**, also called blues rock, emerged in the 1960s. Eric Clapton, the Rolling Stones, and Led Zeppelin are among the most famous blues rockers.

African-American gospel choirs often performed without instrumental accompaniment (or "a cappella"). More people began listening to gospel music when the first radio broadcasts began in the 1920s.

Thomas A. Dorsey (1899–1993) is known as "the Father of Black Gospel Music." Dorsey played piano in vaudeville shows and barrelhouses during the 1920s. He also wrote gospel songs. He started the first black gospel music publishing company, Dorsey House of Music, in 1932. He also founded his own gospel choir and was a founder and first president of the National Convention of Gospel Choirs and Choruses. Two of Dorsey's best-known songs are "Take My Hand, Precious Lord" and "Peace in the Valley." Dorsey helped the careers of many great gospel singers.

One of those singers was Mahalia Jackson (1911–1972). Some people said that Jackson's powerful singing helped them feel closer to God. She made many best-selling records. During the 1950s and 1960s, she was active in the civil rights movement. People call Mahalia Jackson "the Queen of Gospel."

Over the years, there have been many successful gospel singers and groups. Students at an Alabama school for blind African Americans formed a gospel group in 1939. Though the group's membership has changed over the years, it is still around today. In 1992, the Blind Boys of Alabama won a Grammy, the recording industry's most prestigious award. Another gospel group, the Edwin Hawkins Singers, had a crossover hit in 1969 with "Oh Happy Day." The song sold more than 2 million copies.

Mahalia Jackson

Other forms of music were influenced by gospel. These include 1950s-style "doo-wop," which drew on the a cappella sound of gospel. Rhythm and blues (R&B), which became popular in the 1960s, blends gospel and blues.

The great jazz trumpeter and vocalist Louis Armstrong was nicknamed "Satchmo." Jazz used to be mostly group music. Armstrong made instrumental solos and jazz singing more common.

3

JAZZ UP THE MUSIC

In August 2003, President George W. Bush signed into law a bill giving the Smithsonian Institution more funding for its jazz collection. "Jazz," the bill read, "has inspired some of the Nation's leading creative artists and ranks as one of the greatest cultural exports of the United States . . . . Jazz has become an international language that bridges cultural differences and brings people of all races, ages, and backgrounds together." Few people would argue with that assessment.

EARLY JAZZ

Around 1900, people in New Orleans began enjoying a new style of music. This new type of music mixed elements of blues, ragtime, and marching band music. The performers called the music "jass" or "jazz." It was fun music that made people want to dance. At first, New Orleans was the center of jazz. Soon, however, the music spread to other parts of the country. Kansas City, Chicago, and New York all became hot spots of jazz.

In the early days of jazz, groups usually included a "front line" consisting of several musicians who played trumpet, trombone, and clarinet. The front line played the song's melody. The "rhythm section" of a jazz band included musicians playing drums, piano, an upright bass, and often a guitar or banjo.

One important element of jazz music is improvisation—making up musical solos to accompany a song while it is being played. Early jazz groups didn't have sheet music, so all of the performers improvised. Eventually, jazz songs developed structures in which the song's melody was played by one front line instrument (such as the trumpet), while the other front line performers improvised around that melody. Drummers, pianists, and bassists could also be featured in improvisational solos.

The piano player Ferdinand "Jelly Roll" Morton (1885–1941) claimed that he first played jazz as a teenager in 1902. His 1915 song "Jelly Roll Blues" was the first jazz song published as sheet music.

Another important figure in the development of jazz was bandleader Charles "Buddy" Bolden (1877–1931). He played the cornet, a brass instrument similar to the trumpet. His jazz band was the most popular in New Orleans from about 1900 until 1907, when Bolden became mentally ill and could no longer perform. Bolden inspired many other early jazz musicians, including bandleader Joe "King" Oliver (1885–1938). Oliver, in turn, influenced many younger musicians who played with his band.

One of Oliver's most important protégés was Louis Armstrong (1901–1971). Armstrong was a brilliant trumpet player and a master of improvisation. He also was a talented singer with a distinctive voice. His skills helped change the focus of jazz from group music to individual solos. He also helped make jazz singing more common. By the mid-1920s, Armstrong was a major star. He was popular with both black and white audiences. "Satchmo," as he was nicknamed, remained a premier American performer for decades.

THE JAZZ AGE AND THE SWING ERA

In 1920, a new law took effect in the United States. It made the sale of alcohol illegal. From the beginning, however, the law was very unpopular. Americans by and large were in a mood to celebrate. World War I had ended in 1918. The U.S. economy was booming. Increasing numbers of people were moving from rural areas and quiet towns to cities. They want- ed to enjoy the nightlife that cities had to offer, and alcohol was a part of that. Many people went to illegal nightclubs, called speakeasies, where alcohol was served. Often those clubs featured jazz music.

Jazz seemed to perfectly embody the mood of the country during the 1920s. In the United States, in fact, the decade would be called the Jazz Age. Jazz became a symbol of rebellion against the established culture, particularly among young people. Jazz gave rise to fun new dance styles. It was associated with greater social freedom for women.

One famous hot spot of jazz was the Cotton Club, which opened in Harlem in 1923. Many of the greatest African-American musicians played there. For many years Edward "Duke" Ellington (1899–1974) was the leader of the Cotton Club's band. Ellington played piano. He also wrote many hit songs. His band was featured on a weekly radio show. But African Americans couldn't listen to Ellington and his band perform at the Cotton Club. The club was for white patrons only.

During the 1920s and 1930s, groups playing jazz music grew in size. They added more horns, woodwinds, and stringed instruments. These "big bands" usually included 10 to 25 musicians. The big bands didn't improvise nearly as much as had earlier jazz groups. Instead, the bandleader would direct the music and tell performers when they could take a solo.

In 1932, Duke Ellington wrote a song called "It Don't Mean a Thing If It Ain't Got That Swing."

Duke Ellington performs at a club in New York, 1946. In the background is drummer Sonny Greer, who spent many years playing with Ellington's orchestras. Ellington wrote more than 1,000 songs and is considered one of the greatest American music composers of all time.

The song gave a name to the big band style of music: swing. The "swing" in the music referred to the up-tempo rhythm, which made the music great for dancing. From 1935 until the 1950s, swing music was the most popular form of jazz. While African-American musicians had laid the groundwork for swing, white bandleaders enjoyed the greatest commercial success during the swing era. Still, some very popular swing bandleaders were African American. They included Count Basie (1904–1984) and Cab Calloway (1907–1994).

The pianist and bandleader William "Count" Basie (left) leads members of his orchestra in a 1941 performance at the Howard Theater in Washington, D.C. The Count Basie Orchestra was one of the most prominent jazz groups of the "swing" era of the 1930s and 1940s. It employed many great jazz musicians, including the three pictured here: drummer Ray Bauduc, bass player Bob Haggart, and saxophone player Herschel Evans.

Marian Anderson: Singing for Equality

Classical music isn't associated with the African-American experience, as are genres such as blues and jazz. Nevertheless, black performers and composers have made a mark in classical music. One of the most famous was singer Marian Anderson (1897–1993).

By the 1930s, Anderson had won acclaim for her beautiful contralto voice. She had performed with some of the top orchestras in the United States. In 1939, Anderson wanted to perform at Constitution Hall, the largest concert hall in Washington, D.C. But the Daughters of the American Revolution (DAR), which owned Constitution Hall, refused to allow African Americans to perform or attend shows at the venue.

Eleanor Roosevelt, the first lady, was a fan of Anderson's. She helped the singer plan a free outdoor concert on the steps of the Lincoln Memorial. More than 75,000 people—black and white—showed up on Easter Sunday 1939 to hear Anderson sing. Millions more heard the concert on the radio.

Anderson finally got the chance to perform at Constitution Hall on January 7, 1943. Her concert marked the first time the hall had hosted an event at which blacks and whites attended together.

Anderson continued to break racial barriers. In 1955, she became the first African American to perform with the New York Metropolitan Opera.

Anderson lent her voice to the civil rights movement. In 1963, she sang at the landmark March on Washington for Jobs and Freedom. That same year, she was awarded the Presidential Medal of Freedom, the highest civilian honor the U.S. president can bestow.

Marian Anderson

BEBOP

During the 1940s, the form of jazz known as bebop developed. The name probably came from scat, a form of jazz singing in which nonsense words are used in an appealing way. "Bebop" was one of the nonsense words scat artists of the 1920s and 1930s sang.

Bebop was faster than swing. Its melodies were more complicated. It wasn't good dance music because it didn't emphasize a regular beat. Bebop often sounded uneven, with musicians taking wild solos that showed off their individual skill. Bebop was played by small jazz combos. These usually consisted of four or five musicians playing saxophone or trumpet, bass, drums, and piano.

Piano player Thelonious Monk (1917–1982) is sometimes called "the High Priest of Bebop." Other important jazz musicians who helped to

Jazz legends Charlie Parker (sax) and Miles Davis (trumpet) perform at a New York club in 1947. Tommy Potter is the bass player, while Duke Jordan is on the piano.

develop this style included saxophone player Charlie Parker (1920–1955), trumpeter and bandleader Dizzy Gillespie (1917–1993), and drummer Max Roach (1924–2007).

In the mid-1950s, some bebop jazz musicians began to incorporate elements of modern R&B and gospel music into their songs. This style became known as "hard bop." It was particularly popular among musicians performing in New York or the northeastern United States. Performers like trumpeter and composer Miles Davis (1926–1991), bassist and composer Charlie Mingus (1922–1979), saxophone player Julian "Cannonball" Adderley (1928–1975), and pianist/songwriter Horace Silver (b. 1928) made hard bop very popular in the 1950s and 1960s.

> ═ *Did You Know?* ═
>
> The most successful jazz instrumentalists were, until recent times, almost all men. However, many African-American women achieved stardom as jazz vocalists. They included Sarah Vaughan, Ella Fitzgerald, Dinah Washington, and Lena Horne.

COOL JAZZ AND FREE JAZZ

By the late 1940s, some jazz musicians were moving in a stylistic direction away from the high energy and fast tempo of bebop. Their music was calm, smooth, and melodious. The style became known as cool jazz. Although cool jazz originated in New York, the sound was strongly influenced by musicians from the West Coast. Miles Davis and saxophonist Lester Young helped pioneer the cool jazz sound.

Free jazz emerged in the 1950s and 1960s. This experimental music sought to strip jazz of restrictive conventions. Free jazz featured collective, rather than individual, improvisation. Among its pioneers were saxophonist and trumpeter Ornette Coleman, piano player Cecil Taylor, and saxophonist John Coltrane.

In 1997 singer Little Richard was recognized at the American Music Awards ceremony for his contributions to rock 'n' roll music.

THE MODERN BLUES
IGNITES ROCK 'N' ROLL

Blues music has had an enormous impact on rock 'n' roll. Consider the Doors, one of the most popular American rock bands of the late 1960s and early 1970s. Jim Morrison, the group's singer, once confessed that more than half of the music the Doors played was blues.

Across the Atlantic Ocean, one of England's most successful bands might never have come into existence were it not for the blues—or, more specifically, for blues legend Muddy Waters. In 1960, guitarist Keith Richards spotted his high school classmate Mick Jagger on a train. Jagger was carrying the album *The Best of Muddy Waters*. Richards, too, was a fan, and he and Jagger struck up a conversation about the great bluesman.

A couple years later, when the two classmates started a band, they named it after the 1950 Muddy Waters song "Rollin' Stone." Before scoring huge hits with songs such as "(I Can't Get No) Satisfaction," "Paint It Black," and "Ruby Tuesday," the Rolling Stones covered songs by Muddy Waters, Howlin' Wolf, and other blues artists. Much of the Stones' later work would also retain a blues feel.

THE MODERN BLUES

In 1943, McKinley Morganfield moved from his native Mississippi to Chicago. There, the 30-year-old guitar player began calling himself Muddy Waters. He added electric guitar, drums, harmonica, and upright bass to the Delta blues. In the process, he changed the blues. Modern blues was more upbeat and fun. Some people didn't approve. They thought the blues should always be about hard times.

Blues great B. B. King disagreed. He thought blues music could make you happy. "The blues," King said, "isn't just about being blue; that's just a name they gave it, just like every rock 'n' roll tune I've heard wasn't rock 'n' roll."

King, who was born in 1925, got his start in music as a child in Mississippi. He played guitar on street corners for small change. King released his first album, *Singin' the Blues*, in 1956. More than 50 albums would follow, and King remains popular today.

During the late 1940s and early 1950s, many American radio stations were playing modern blues. But musicians like Chuck Berry, Bo Diddley, Fats Domino, and Little Richard changed the music, paving the way for a new genre. "The blues," Little Richard would say, "had a baby and they named it rock 'n' roll."

The legendary blues guitarist B. B. King (b. 1925) influenced many of the great electric guitar players of rock 'n' roll, including Jimi Hendrix, Eric Clapton, Robert Cray, and Stevie Ray Vaughan. In 1987, B. B. King was inducted into the Rock and Roll Hall of Fame.

THE BIRTH OF ROCK 'N' ROLL

Rock 'n' roll mixes rhythm and blues, pop, country and western, and gospel music. Some rhythm and blues records from the 1920s sound like rock 'n' roll. And many early rock 'n' roll songs from the 1950s were covers of blues tunes African Americans had recorded earlier.

Music historians disagree on which song should be considered the first true rock 'n' roll recording. Some candidates are "Good Rockin' Tonight" by Wynonie Harris (1947); "Rock the Joint" (1949) by Jimmy Preston; "Rocket 88" by Jackie Brenston and Ike Turner (1951); and "Shake, Rattle, and Roll" by Big Joe Turner (1954). All of these artists were African Americans.

But rock 'n' roll gained mainstream popularity only when white artists began working in the genre. In 1954, Bill Haley and the Comets released "Rock Around the Clock," and Elvis Presley released "That's All Right (Mama)." Both records would frequently be cited as the first true rock 'n' roll song. Had the pioneering contributions of African Americans been overlooked?

For his part, Presley had little doubt. His "That's All Right" was a cover of a song by the African-American singer, songwriter, and guitarist Arthur "Big Boy" Crudup. "The colored folks been singing [rock 'n' roll] and playing it just like

Nat King Cole was a renowned vocalist when the NBC television network tapped him to host a variety show. The *Nat King Cole Show*, which debuted in November 1956 and ran for 64 weeks, marked the first time an African-American entertainer had hosted a network variety show.

I'm doing now, man, for more years than I know," Presley noted in 1956. "I got it from them. Down in Tupelo, Mississippi, I used to hear old Arthur Crudup bang his [guitar] the way I do now, and I said if I ever got to the place where I could feel all old Arthur felt, I'd be a music man like nobody ever saw." In time, Presley would be a music man like nobody ever saw. Dubbed "the King of Rock 'n' Roll," he became one of the most successful recording artists of all time.

BLACK ROCKERS

Ironically, the popularity of early white rockers—who were drawing heavily on African-American influences—helped pave the way for black artists to achieve mainstream success in rock 'n' roll. One of these black artists was Chuck Berry (born 1926). Berry mixed the sounds of country guitar and rhythm and blues. He sang about subjects that teenagers liked, such as cars, girls, and school. Berry scored hits with songs such as "Maybellene" (1955), "Johnny B. Goode" (1958), and "No Particular Place to Go" (1964). He would greatly influence many later rockers.

Little Richard, born Richard Wayne Penniman in 1932, was another influential African-American rock 'n' roll star. Hits such as "Tutti Frutti" (1955), "Long Tall Sally" (1956), and "Good Golly Miss Molly" (1958)—along with a manic stage presence—made him popular with young people of all backgrounds. At a time when Jim Crow laws were still in effect in the South, black and white fans mixed freely at Little Richard's concerts.

= Did You Know? =

Doo-wop was a popular form of rhythm and blues in the 1950s. Doo-wop hits included "Sh-Boom" by the Chords, "Earth Angel" by the Penguins, and "In the Still of the Night" by the Five Satins.

As a teenager, Bo Diddley (1928–2008)—whose given name was Ellas Otha Bates—learned to play the violin and trombone. But, dazzled by the artistry of bluesmen John Lee Hooker and Muddy Waters, he took up the guitar. Playing his trademark rectangular guitar, Diddley delighted fans with such favorites as "Who Do You Love?" and "I'm a Man." His songs were widely covered.

The Coasters were among the first African-American groups to sing rock 'n' roll. They burst onto the scene with 1957's "Young Blood." Other hits included "Yakety Yak" (1958) and "Charlie Brown" (1959), which both were humorous songs.

Piano player Antoine "Fats" Domino, born in 1928, got his start in boogie-woogie music. In 1955, he released his first album, *Carry on Rockin'*. Over the next 10 years, he scored numerous rock and pop hits.

In the mid-1960s, rock music in the United States was transformed by the so-called British invasion. Groups from England—such as the Beatles, the Kinks, the Animals, and the Rolling Stones—burst onto the American music charts. Many of the British invasion bands drew inspiration from earlier African-American music, especially the blues.

By the late 1960s, almost all of the top rock acts were white. One notable exception was Jimi Hendrix (1942–1970). Widely regarded as the best rock guitarist of all time, Hendrix was completely self-taught. His style was unique and innovative. Hendrix pioneered the use of feedback on the electric guitar.

Hendrix's career was brief. Only three studio albums, all with his trio the Jimi Hendrix Experience, were released during his lifetime. But those albums—*Are You Experienced* (1967), *Axis: Bold as Love* (1967), and *Electric Ladyland* (1968)—were hugely influential. And Hendrix's performance at the Woodstock Music Festival in 1969, particularly his searing rendition of "The Star-Spangled Banner," is the stuff of musical legend.

Hendrix died at age 27, probably from the effects of an overdose of sleeping pills. But his music continues to influence musicians today, more than 40 years later.

Singer and entertainer James Brown (1933–2006) was known as the "Godfather of Soul," but he had a strong influence on many musical genres, including rock, funk, and R&B.

5

OF R&B, SOUL, AND FUNK

If white musicians dominated mainstream rock 'n' roll by the late 1960s, African-American artists were by then exploring other musical currents. They included rhythm and blues, soul, and funk.

RHYTHM AND BLUES

Rhythm and blues, or R&B, first developed during the early 1940s. The sound was a mix of jazz, gospel, and blues, with quiet singing and an easy rhythm. Many of the songs were about love. The African-American saxophone player and bandleader Louis Jordan (1908–1975) was a pioneer in the genre, which was initially classified under the category "race records." That term referred to any music marketed to African Americans. In 1949, however, *Billboard* magazine—the American music industry's leading trade publication—created a rhythm & blues chart. The music would gain more crossover success without any reference to race.

African-American R&B stars of the 1950s included Roy Brown (1925–1981), Ruth Brown (1928–2006), Della Reese (born 1931), and Frankie Lymon (1942–1968). Later performers who recorded R&B or were deeply influenced by it include Marvin Gaye, Wilson Pickett, Smokey

Louis Jordan was one of the most popular and successful bandleaders of the 1940s and 1950s. His method of blending jazz and blues contributed to the development of both the rock 'n' roll and R&B genres during the 1950s.

Robinson, Michael Jackson, Whitney Houston, Prince, and Tina Turner. Many of these stars also performed soul music.

SOUL

Soul music, which blends R&B with a strong gospel sound, began emerging in the early 1960s. Detroit, Memphis, and Chicago were early centers of this genre, and each produced a characteristic sound. Detroit soul had a polished sound with simple and clear vocals. Memphis soul was closer to pure blues. Chicago soul was a mix of the Detroit and Memphis varieties. The artists who pioneered soul included James Brown, Ray Charles, and Sam Cooke.

Brown (1933–2006) was known as "the Godfather of Soul" and "Soul Brother Number One," among other nicknames. He was a singer and multi-instrumentalist with a well-earned reputation for highly energetic live performances. Brown's best-known songs include "Papa's Got a Brand New Bag" and "I Got You (I Feel Good)", both released in 1965. The 1968 hit "Say It Loud—I'm Black and I'm Proud" became an anthem for African-American empowerment.

Ray Charles Robinson (1930–2004) shortened his name to Ray Charles because he didn't want to be confused with the champion boxer Sugar Ray Robinson. Charles started losing his sight at an early age. He was completely blind by age seven. Still, he managed to master the piano. He was also an accomplished composer and vocalist who won acclaim in a variety of musical genres. "As a musician, Ray Charles was unmatched," noted the famous producer Quincy Jones. "A musical genius who made every song he performed his own. There will never be another musician who did as much to break down the perceived walls of musical genres as much as Ray Charles did."

Sam Cooke (1931–1964) sang gospel before scoring an R&B hit with 1957's "You Send Me." He used the money he made from that song to cofound SAR Records. The label featured soul artists. Cooke himself didn't record for SAR, but he wrote and sang a series of soul and R&B hits for other labels. They included "Chain Gang" (1960), "Wonderful World" (1960), and "Twistin' the Night Away" (1962).

Two giants of soul music would emerge later in the 1960s. Otis Redding was just 26 years old when he died in a December 1967 plane crash. But his song "Respect" (1965) had already become a soul classic. "(Sittin' On) The Dock of the Bay," released a month after Redding's death, quickly rocketed to the top of the Billboard pop charts.

Aretha Franklin, born in 1942, burst onto the music scene with a 1967 cover of Redding's "Respect." Her version spoke powerfully to the issue of women's rights. So did "Think," a soul hit from 1968. In her long career, Franklin has 45 Top 40 hits to her credit, along with 10 number-one R&B albums.

A few other notable soul artists from the 1960s and 1970s are Booker

Ray Charles (1930–2004) blended gospel, jazz, blues, and R&B to create music that was popular with both black and white audiences. He had many hits during the 1950s and 1960s, including "What'd I Say," "Hit the Road, Jack," "I Can't Stop Loving You," and "Georgia on my Mind."

T. & the MG's, Percy Sledge, and Sam and Dave. More recently, Mary J. Blige, Anthony Hamilton, and the British artist Joss Stone have worked in the genre.

THAT MOTOWN SOUND

In 1959, a part-time songwriter and aspiring music producer named Berry Gordy Jr. launched his own record label, Tamla, in his hometown of Detroit. Gordy's initial outlay was just $800. From that modest beginning, Gordy's label—whose name was changed to Motown in 1960—would grow to the largest African-American–owned business of any kind by the 1970s.

Motown would also play an outsized role in the history of American pop music. It launched the careers of a host of major African-American recording stars and groups. A partial list includes Smokey Robinson & the Miracles, Diana Ross & the Supremes, the Four Tops, the Temptations, Marvin Gaye, Stevie Wonder, Gladys Knight & the Pips, the Jackson Five, and Michael Jackson. To an extent never before seen, Motown achieved crossover success with African-American music. Whites as well as blacks loved the Motown sound, which featured ear-catching melodies, powerful bass lines, an abundance of horns, and strong percussion sections. Motown lyrics were invariably polished yet catchy.

Motown's artists notched numerous chart-topping hits and sold millions upon millions of records. More important, their music helped break down racial barriers. "I would come to the South in the early days of Motown and the audiences would be segregated," recalled Smokey Robinson. "Then they started to get the Motown music and we would go back and the audiences were integrated and the kids were dancing together and holding hands."

═ Did You Know? ═

Stevie Wonder recorded his 1981 song "Happy Birthday" as part of a campaign to make the birthday of civil rights leader Martin Luther King Jr. a national holiday. President Ronald Reagan signed the King Holiday Bill into law in November 1983.

One of the most popular Motown groups of the 1960s and 1970s was the Jackson Five (rght); young singer Michael Jackson (pictured second from right) would go on to a spectacular solo career. Motown Records founder Berry Gordy (below, left) helped to launch the careers of such superstars as Diana Ross, Smokey Robinson, and Stevie Wonder.

FUNK

By the 1970s, the popularity of soul music had crested. Funk was at the cutting edge of African-American music. Early funk blended jazz, blues, and soul influences. It emphasized rhythm over melody and had a driving bass line, which made it good dance music. Later funk would often incorporate reggae and Latin music.

Funk got its name from crowds in African-American clubs. People sometimes shouted "Funk" to make the band play harder. Who deserves the credit for pioneering funk? As with questions about the origins of other musical genres, that is difficult to answer. Some people say Little Richard's band had a funk vibe in the 1950s. Others insist that James Brown's "Out of Sight," released in 1964, was the first true funk song. Certainly both

The innovative musician George Clinton (b. 1941) pioneered the funk musical genre during the 1970s.

men helped shape the genre.

Sly and the Family Stone, a band that formed in 1967, helped separate funk from soul. Two other groups, Kool and the Gang (formed in 1969) and Earth, Wind & Fire (formed in 1971) would also make notable contributions to funk.

However, no one is more associated with funk than George Clinton. During the 1970s, Clinton led two popular funk bands: Parliament and Funkadelic. The two bands started out playing different kinds of funk. But they were made up of many of the same musicians, and the differences in their respective sounds became hard to identify. As a result, many fans came to refer to one band: Parliament-Funkadelic, or P-Funk. In addition to its funk sounds, P-Funk was known for crazy onstage stunts. By the early 1980s, P-Funk had dissolved, and funk's heyday was over.

Still, Clinton's projects would influence bands such as Living Colour and the Red Hot Chili Peppers. Funk would also be sampled by many hip-hop artists. Dr. Dre's pioneering G-funk (gangsta funk) sound would make especially effective use of Parliament-Funkadelic's work.

Charley Pride

Country music isn't known as a genre in which African Americans have starred. Charley Pride is a notable exception.

Pride, born in Mississippi in 1938, taught himself to play guitar as a young teen. He first dreamed of a career in professional baseball. He played on several teams in the Negro leagues, as well as farm clubs of Major League Baseball's New York Yankees and Cincinnati Reds. During bus trips, Pride would entertain his teammates by strumming on his guitar and singing. When his baseball dreams failed to pan out, he thought of a career in music.

In 1965, Pride signed a recording contract with RCA Records. The following year, RCA released three singles from the artist it billed as "Country Charley Pride." This was a time of significant racial unrest in the United States, and country had long been regarded as a "white" genre. So no photos of Pride were released, and no mention of his race was made.

By 1967, Pride's song "Just Between You and Me" had cracked the top 10 on the Billboard country singles chart. That year, Pride performed onstage at the Grand Ole Opry in Nashville. Country fans seemed not to care about his race.

Between 1969 and 1971, Pride notched eight number-one country singles (today his career total stands at 29). In 1971, he won the Country Music Association's Entertainer of the Year and Male Vocalist of the Year awards. He took home Male Vocalist of the Year honors again in 1972.

Charley Pride was elected to the Country Music Hall of Fame in 2000.

Charley Pride

Brooklyn-born rapper Shawn "Jay-Z" Carter is considered one of the biggest hip-hop stars of the 1990s and 2000s.

6

HIP-HOP AND BEYOND

In November 1982, Michael Jackson's sixth studio album was released. The 24-year-old singer, songwriter, and dancer was already popular. But *Thriller* catapulted him to heights of success never before seen in the music industry. The album spawned seven top 10 singles. It won a record-setting eight Grammys. And it would become the top-selling album in history. Michael Jackson became the undisputed "King of Pop." He was the biggest star in the United States. He was also a worldwide phenomenon, with legions of fans all over the globe. "In the world of pop music," the *New York Times* noted, "there is Michael Jackson and there is everybody else."

While Jackson was hailed as the biggest pop star on the face of earth, another kind of music was just beginning to emerge into the mainstream. For about a decade it had been developing in African-American neighborhoods, first in New York City and then, a bit later, in Los Angeles. Relatively few people outside of those areas knew much if anything about hip-hop. But soon this music would take the United States—and the world—by storm.

HIP-HOP BEGINNINGS

Hip-hop was born in the South Bronx section of New York City during the early 1970s. Numerous influences and individuals contributed to the development of hip-hop. But DJ Kool Herc and Afrika Bambaataa deserve special mention.

As a teen, Kool Herc, born Clive Campbell in Jamaica in 1955, hosted dance and block parties in his South Bronx neighborhood. He played a lot of funk music. Herc found that people liked to dance the most during percussion sections of the songs. As a DJ, he began playing only these sections, known as "breaks." Herc often had two copies of the songs he played, one for each of his two turntables. As a break was coming to an end, he would switch to the other turntable, where the beginning of the break was cued up. In this way, he could effectively loop a break for as long as he wanted.

As of 2012, Quincy Jones had received a record 79 Grammy nominations and won 27 times.

Herc also used his fingers to move a record back and forth on the turntable. This technique, known as scratching, produced interesting new sounds. Scratching would become a mainstay of hip-hop DJing.

At Herc's dance and block parties, people would gather in a circle while dancers called B-boys (and later, B-girls) tried to outdo one another by performing difficult and acrobatic solo dance moves. (The mainstream media would refer to this as "break dancing," although that term wasn't used in hip-hop culture.) As the B-boys and B-girls were dancing, Herc would MC—rapping about the scene with improvised rhymes.

Other young DJs saw Herc in action

and were influenced by his style. One of
them was Afrika Bambaataa. Bambaataa,
born in the South Bronx in 1960, had seen
his neighborhood ravaged by violent street
gangs. He thought the emerging hip-hop
culture could provide an alternative to gang
life. Instead of fighting rivals over turf,
African-American youth could compete
with one another—and ultimately come
together—through rapping and B-boying.
Bambaataa formed a youth group in the
South Bronx to promote his vision. Other
DJs helped, and the idea worked. "For over
five years the Bronx had lived in constant
terror of street gangs," wrote journalist
Steven Hager. "Suddenly, in 1975, they dis-
appeared almost as quickly as they had
arrived. This happened because something
better came along to replace the gangs.
That something was eventually called hip-
hop."

During the 1980s and 1990s, pop
singer Whitney Houston
(1963–2012) was one of the biggest
stars in American music.

During the late 1970s, hip-hop DJs and MCs became local celebrities
in New York. They worked dance clubs in addition to block and house parties. Individual DJs and MCs developed their own loyal fan bases.

By 1979, a hip-hop scene had also begun developing in Los Angeles.
But it was a New York–based group, the Fatback Band, that released what
many critics consider the first hip-hop single. Released in August 1979,
"King Tim III (Personality Jock)" didn't sell very well. Another hip-hop
song, released just a few weeks later, fared a bit better. The Sugarhill
Gang's disco-infused "Rapper's Delight" reached #36 on the Billboard Hot
100 pop singles chart. This modest success hinted at the commercial
potential of hip-hop music.

INTO THE MAINSTREAM

The first half of the 1980s saw the emergence of numerous hip-hop acts. Many of them recorded a single or two and promptly faded into obscurity. From the standpoint of production, much of the hip-hop music released during this early period was fairly simple. In terms of content, a lot of early hip-hop can be classified as party music, with light themes such as infatuation or the joys of hanging out. A significant exception was "The Message," a 1982 single from Grandmaster Flash and the Furious Five. It presented a stark picture of life in the ghetto.

The self-titled debut album of Run-D.M.C., released in 1984, signaled new directions for hip-hop. On *Run-D.M.C.*, the New York–based trio of Jam-Master Jay, D.M.C., and Reverend Run set a high bar for swagger. They rapped about the superiority of their own skills. They taunted other hip-hop artists. And musically, hard rock influences could be heard on the album. This mixing of genres would be more fully

> — *Did You Know?* —
>
> Run-D.M.C. was the first hip-hop group to sing on MTV, and the first to appear on the cover of *Rolling Stone* magazine.

realized with Run-D.M.C.'s next albums, *King of Rock* (1985) and *Raising Hell* (1986). The latter included a cover of Aerosmith's 1975 rock classic "Walk This Way"—complete with performances by Steven Tyler and Joe Perry of Aerosmith. The single reached #4 on the Billboard Hot 100 pop chart. *Raising Hell* peaked at #3 on the Billboard 200 albums chart, and it was the first hip-hop album ever to achieve platinum status (one million copies sold). Hip-hop had achieved crossover success.

Meanwhile, hip-hop on the West Coast was evolving into hard-core gangsta rap. Pioneering albums included *Rhyme Pays* (1987), by Ice-T; *Straight Outta Compton* (1988), by N.W.A.; and Dr. Dre's *The Chronic* (1992). Gangsta rap spotlighted subjects such as drug abuse, crime, and violence against women. Many critics said it glorified bad behavior.

Andre "Dr. Dre" Young (right) with his protégé Snoop Dogg. The two hip-hop stars collaborated to produce two of the most popular albums of the 1990s: Dre's *The Chronic* (1992) and Snoop's *Doggystyle* (1993).

But West Coast gangsta rap—especially that released by Los Angeles–based Death Row Records—was extremely popular with fans. It also received acclaim from many music critics. Much of that success can be credited to the production genius of Dr. Dre. He brought a musical intricacy to hip-hop. Dre tapped many genres (which would become a hallmark of much hip-hop that followed) and introduced new techniques. The Dre-produced album *Doggystyle*, the 1993 debut of rapper Snoop Doggy Dogg, was a case in point. "Dre's production takes hip-hop to another

In 2001, Beyoncé Knowles became the first African-American woman to win the Songwriter of the Year award from the American Society of Composers, Authors and Publishers (ASCAP).

level," wrote a music critic for the *Los Angeles Times*, "organic yet relentless, the air alive with sleigh bells, sighs, countermelodies, wisps of Temptations-style backing vocals and low-mixed call-and-response that seems to float in from the ether." *Doggystyle* became the first hip-hop album ever to enter the Billboard 200 pop charts at #1. Within two months, it had sold an amazing 3 million copies.

Tupac Shakur would notch even bigger sales with two albums he recorded for Death Row. *All Eyez on Me* had sold 5 million copies within two months of its February 1996 release. *The Don Killuminati: The 7 Day Theory*, released two months after Tupac's murder in September 1996, sold 4 million copies.

CONTINUING APPEAL

In the late 1990s, Missy Elliott and Lauryn Hill proved that male rappers had no monopoly on hip-hop stardom. Elliott's debut album, *Supa Dupa Fly* (1997), went platinum. *Da Real World*, released in 1999, also sold more than a million copies.

Hill, a member of the hip-hop/soul trio the Fugees, released her debut solo album, *The Miseducation of Lauryn Hill*, in 1998. It shot to number one on the Billboard 200 albums chart and eventually sold more than 8 million copies. Hill garnered five Grammys, including Album of the Year and Best New Artist honors.

Stars like Jay-Z, Beyoncé, 50 Cent, and Kanye West have kept hip-hop at the top of the American music charts in the 21st century. And hip-hop has been embraced by hundreds of millions of music fans all over the globe. It has influenced and enriched the popular music of dozens of countries. All of this confirms the powerful legacy of African-American musicians—who have played such an important role in giving the world blues, jazz, gospel, soul, R&B, and rock 'n' roll.

Spanning the generations: current hip-hop star Curtis "50 Cent" Jackson (right) poses with Motown Records legend Smokey Robinson at the 2011 NAACP Image Awards ceremony.

CHAPTER NOTES

p. 11: "Music can tell a story . . . ." Barack Obama, Presidential Proclamation—African-American Music Appreciation Month, May 28, 2010. http://www.whitehouse.gov/the-press-office/presidential-proclamation-african-american-music-appreciation-month

p. 20: "the weirdest music . . ." W. C. Handy, quoted on PBS's "The Blues," at http://www.pbs.org/theblues/classroom/essaysblues.html

p. 22: "the finest music . . ." Eric Clapton, liner notes for *Me and Mr. Johnson* by Eric Clapton. Reprise Records/Warner Music Group, 2004.

p. 27: "Jazz has inspired . . ." H. R. 2195, 108th Congress of the United States of America (January 7, 2003), available at http://www.gov-track.us/congress/billtext.xpd?bill=h108-2195

p. 36: "The blues isn't just . . ." B. B. King, quoted in Gary Graff, "B. B. King," *Billboard* vol. 117, issue 40 (October 1, 2005), pp. 35-40.

p. 36: "The blues had a baby . . . " Little Richard, quoted in Kevin Chappell, "How Blacks Invented Rock and Roll: R&B Stars Created Foundations of Multibillion-dollar Music Industry," *Ebony* (January 1997). http://findarticles.com/p/articles/mi_m1077/is_n3_v52/ai_18980636/

p. 37: "The colored folks . . ." Christopher John Farley, "Elvis Rocks. But He's Not the First," *Time* (July 6, 2004). http://www.time.com/time/arts/article/0,8599,661084,00.html

p. 42: "As a musician, Ray Charles . . . " Quincy Jones, quoted in "Celebrities Share How They Will Remember Ray Charles," *Jet* vol. 105, issue 26 (June 28, 2004), pp. 62–64.

p. 44: "I would come to the South . . ." Smokey Robinson, quoted in Ron Thibodeaux, "My Smokey Valentine," *(New Orleans) Times-Picayune*, February 14, 2009.

p. 48: "In the world of pop . . ." Jon Pareles, "Michael Jackson at 25: A Musical Phenomenon," *New York Times*, January 14, 1984, Section 1, p. 11.

p. 51:   "For over five years . . ." Steven Hager, "Afrika Bambaataa's Hip-Hop," in *And It Didn't Stop?: The Best American Hip-Hop Journalism of the Last 25 Years*, edited by Raquel Cepeda (New York: Farrar, Straus and Giroux: 2004), p. 18.

p. 53:   "Dre's production takes . . ." Jonathan Gold, "Snoop Doggy Dogg: A 'Style, All His Own," *Los Angeles Times*, November 21, 1993. http://articles.latimes.com/1993-11-21/entertainment/ca-59113_1_point-snoop-doggy-dogg

R&B singer Kanye West, shown here performing in Gothenburg, Sweden, in 2011, has become an international music star.

CHRONOLOGY

1865	The Civil War ends, and all African-American slaves are freed.
1871	The Fisk Jubilee Singers begin a concert tour of the United States to raise money for Fisk University.
1893	Scott Joplin performs at the Chicago World's Fair, helping to introduce ragtime music to a wide audience.
1903	W. C. Handy, "Father of the Blues," hears a man singing and playing a new kind of music. Handy uses the style to develop the blues.
1917	The first recording of a jazz song—"Darktown Strutter's Ball" by the Original Dixieland Jazz Band—is made.
1920	Mamie Smith's "Crazy Blues" becomes the first blues song to be recorded.
1926	Blind Lemon Jefferson becomes the first blues artist to record a solo album for a major studio.
1928	Clarence "Pinetop" Smith records "Pinetop's Boogie-Woogie."
1939	Denied the opportunity to perform at Constitution Hall in Washington, D.C., singer Marian Anderson gives a free concert in front of the Lincoln Memorial. More than 75,000 attend, and millions listen to the radio broadcast.
1959	Berry Gordy Jr. founds the label that will become Motown Records.
1967	Otis Redding dies in a plane crash. Aretha Franklin scores her first hit with a cover of Redding's song "Respect."
1971	Charley Pride becomes the first African American to win the Country Music Association's Entertainer of the Year award.
1979	The Sugarhill Gang's song "Rapper's Delight" helps make rap popular.
1982	Michael Jackson's *Thriller* is released. It becomes the best-selling album of all time.
1986	Run-D.M.C. releases *Raising Hell*, which becomes the first hip-hop album to sell a million copies.
1993	Snoop Doggy Dogg's *Doggystyle* becomes the first hip-hop album ever to enter the Billboard 200 album chart at #1.
2010	On May 28, Barack Obama signs a Presidential Proclamation to make June 2010 African-American Music Appreciation Month.

GLOSSARY

combo—a group of at least three jazz musicians.

crossover—appealing to or enjoying commercial success with fans of more than one genre.

discrimination—the act of treating some people better than others for an unfair reason like race or ethnic background.

genre—a category of artistic expression, such as a particular kind of music (for example, blues or rock 'n' roll).

improvise—in music, to create part of a song (such as an instrumental solo) spontaneously, in the middle of a performance.

Jim Crow laws—laws, in effect in the South from the late 1800s to the mid-1900s, that kept African Americans from using the same public facilities as whites.

lyrics—the words of a song.

racism—a discrimination or prejudice based on a person's race; the belief that one race of people is superior to another.

segregation—the practice of keeping one group or race separated from another.

troupe—a group of traveling performers.

vaudeville—a type of stage show popular in the late 1880s and early 1900s that included singers, dancers, comedians, and other acts.

FURTHER READING

Blumenthal, Bob. *Jazz: An Introduction to the History and Legends Behind America's Music*. London: HarperCollins, 2007.

Freedman, Russell. *The Voice That Challenged a Nation: Marian Anderson and the Struggle for Equal Rights*. New York: Clarion Books, 2004.

Giovanni, Nikki. *On My Journey Now: Looking at African-American History Through the Spirituals*. Somerville, MA: Candlewick, 2009.

Guralnick, Peter. *Sweet Soul Music: Rhythm and Blues and the Southern Dream of Freedom*. New York: Harper & Row, 1986.

Phinney, Kevin. *Souled American: How Black Music Transformed White Culture*. New York: Billboard Books, 2005.

Southern, Eileen. *The Music of Black Americans: A History*, 3rd edition. New York: W. W. Norton & Co., 1997.

Stewart, Earl L. *African American Music: An Introduction*. New York: Schirmer Books, 1998.

INTERNET RESOURCES

http://www.carnegiehall.org/honor/history/index.aspx

This site, which presents the history of African-American music, includes information about genres, biographies of important artists, an interactive timeline, and more.

http://www.pbs.org/jazz

The companion website for the PBS documentary *Jazz*, by acclaimed filmmaker Ken Burns.

http://www.pbs.org/theblues

This website includes a wealth of information about blues music and artists. It is the companion site for the seven-part PBS series *The Blues*.

http://www.pbs.org/wgbh/amex/foster/sfeature/sf_minstrelsy.html

An informative page on blackface minstrelsy, part of the PBS *American Experience* program about composer Stephen Foster.

http://www.soul-patrol.com

This site features information about soul albums and artists, as well as blues, doo-wop, funk, jazz, rock, and other kinds of music.

INDEX

Numbers in **bold italics** refer to captions.

CONTRIBUTORS

CLAUDETTE HEGEL is the author of more than 250 publications for children and adults. Her seven books include four books for teachers and media center specialists, biographies of Randolph Caldecott and John Newbery, and a book about tigers for children. The sounds of blues, jazz, and soul artists often surround Claudette and her cat, Mewsic, in their home in Bloomington, Minnesota.

Senior Consulting Editor **DR. MARC LAMONT HILL** is one of the leading hip-hop generation intellectuals in the country. Dr. Hill has lectured widely and provides regular commentary for media outlets like NPR, the *Washington Post, Essence Magazine*, the *New York Times*, CNN, MSNBC, and *The O'Reilly Factor*. He is the host of the nationally syndicated television show *Our World With Black Enterprise*. Dr. Hill is a columnist and editor-at-large for the *Philadelphia Daily News*. His books include the award-winning *Beats, Rhymes, and Classroom Life: Hip-Hop Pedagogy and the Politics of Identity* (2009).

Since 2009 Dr. Hill has been on the faculty of Columbia University as Associate Professor of Education at Teachers College. He holds an affiliated faculty appointment in African American Studies at the Institute for Research in African American Studies at Columbia University.

Since his days as a youth in Philadelphia, Dr. Hill has been a social justice activist and organizer. He is a founding board member of My5th, a non-profit organization devoted to educating youth about their legal rights and responsibilities. He is also a board member and organizer of the Philadelphia Student Union. Dr. Hill also works closely with the ACLU Drug Reform Project, focusing on drug informant policy. In addition to his political work, Dr. Hill continues to work directly with African American and Latino youth.

In 2005, *Ebony* named Dr. Hill one of America's 100 most influential Black leaders. The magazine had previously named him one of America's top 30 Black leaders under 30 years old.